Pebble™ Plus

Animal Offspring

Dogs and Their Puppies

by Linda Tagliaferro

Consulting Editor: Gail Saunders-Smith, Ph.D.
Consultant: Martin Deeley, President
International Association of Canine Professionals
Montverde, Florida

Capstone press

Mankato, Minnesota

Pebble Plus is published by Capstone Press
151 Good Counsel Drive, P.O. Box 669, Mankato, Minnesota 56002
http://www.capstonepress.com

1 2 3 4 5 6 09 08 07 06 05 04

Library of Congress Cataloging-in-Publication Data
Tagliaferro, Linda.
Dogs and their puppies/by Linda Tagliaferro.
p. cm.—(Pebble plus: Animal offspring)
Contents—Dogs—Puppies—Growing up—Watch dogs grow.
Includes bibliographical references and index.
ISBN 0-7368-2388-3 (hardcover)
1. Puppies—Juvenile literature. 2. Dogs—Juvenile literature. 3. Parental behavior in animals—Juvenile
literature. [1. Dogs. 2. Animals—Infancy. 3. Parental behavior in animals.] I. Title. II. Series.
SF426.5T34 2004
636.7′07—dc21   2003008489

Editorial Credits
Sarah L. Schuette, editor; Kia Adams, series designer; Kelly Garvin and Deirdre Barton, photo researchers;
    Karen Risch, product planning editor

Photo Credits
Bruce Coleman Inc./John Daniels, 20 (left)
Cheryl A. Ertelt, 15, 16–17
Corbis, 4–5; LWA-Dann Tardif, 10–11; Renee Lynn, 7
Jack Macfarlane, 9, 12–13
Mark Raycroft, 18–19, 20 (right), 21 (all)
Minden Pictures/Mitsuaki Wago, cover
Photoalto/Jean-Louis Aubert, 1

Note to Parents and Teachers

The Animal Offspring series supports national science standards related to life science.
This book describes and illustrates dogs and their puppies. The images support early
readers in understanding the text. The repetition of words and phrases helps early
readers learn new words. This book also introduces early readers to subject-specific
vocabulary words, which are defined in the Glossary section. Early readers may need
assistance to read some words and to use the Table of Contents, Glossary, Read More,
Internet Sites, and Index/Word List sections of the book.

Word Count: 86
Early-Intervention Level: 12

1.4

Table of Contents

Dogs

Dogs are mammals.
Young dogs are
called puppies.

Male and female dogs mate.

Female dogs give birth

to a litter of puppies.

Puppies

Puppies cannot see
or hear until they are
about ten days old.

Puppies sleep most of
the time. Puppies get tired
from playing.

Puppies drink milk from their mother for about five weeks.

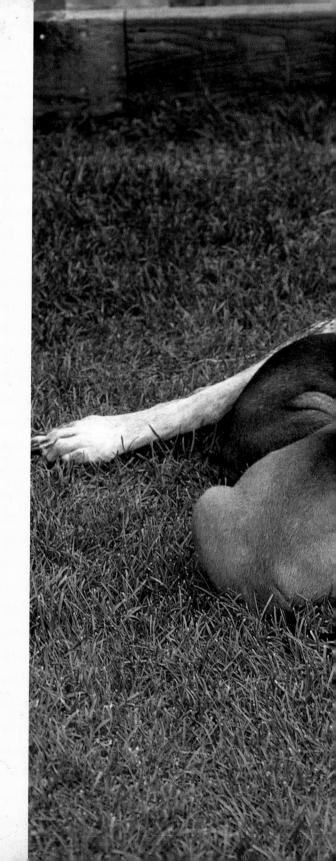

Growing Up

Puppies can eat dog food when they are about six weeks old.

Puppies jump on and
play with each other.
They chew toys.

Puppies become adults
after one to two years.

Watch Dogs Grow

birth _____

**adult after one
to two years**

Glossary

adult—an animal that is able to mate

litter—a group of puppies born at the same time to the same mother; dogs usually have litters of four to six puppies.

mammal—a warm-blooded animal that has a backbone; most mammals have hair or fur; female mammals feed milk to their young.

mate—to join together to produce young

Read More

Anderson, J. I. *I Can Read About Dogs and Puppies.* Mahwah, N.J.: Troll, 2001.

Macken, JoAnn Early. *Puppies.* Let's Read About Pets. Milwaukee: Weekly Reader Early Learning, 2003.

Trumbauer, Lisa. *The Life Cycle of a Dog.* Life Cycles. Mankato, Minn.: Pebble Books, 2002.

Internet Sites

FactHound offers a safe, fun way to find Internet sites related to this book. All of the sites on FactHound have been researched by our staff.

Here's how:

1. Visit *www.facthound.com*

2. Type in this special code **0736823883** for age-appropriate sites or enter a search word related to this book for a more general search..

3. Click on the Fetch It button.

FactHound will fetch the best sites for you!

Index/Word List